The Portage Series

Series Titles

Careful Cartography
Devon Bohm

Broken On the Wheel
Barbara Costas-Biggs

Sparks and Disperses
Cathleen Cohen

Holding My Selves Together: New and Selected Poems
Margaret Rozga

Lost and Found Departments
Heather Dubrow

Marginal Notes
Alfonso Brezmes

The Almost-Children
Cassondra Windwalker

Meditations of a Beast
Kristine Ong Muslim

Praise for
Devon Bohm

There is in this book an articulate, on-rushing breathlessness that speaks to and for the self's response to the feast of life. The hazards are many—and they are scrupulously noted. Bohm is, among other things, an itinerant moralist, yet one who again and again returns to the compelling force—sometimes felt with other people and sometimes on her own—of being here on earth in the great, confusing vortex of Now. She conveys that force in a myriad of poetic approaches, many long-lined, all replete with detailed energy that keeps the reader engaged and something like enthralled—this is a life that speaks for many lives.

—Baron Wormser,
author of *Legends of the Slow Explosion*

Devon Bohm's *Careful Cartography* is both those things, but like all good map makers, the poet is committed not only to the known but the unknown, the places at the edge of the map that resist nomenclature. It's to those tendernesses most prone to grief, longing, and loss that the cartographer-poet turns our attention, acknowledging, as she does, that the real uncharted territory is that which is interior. It's slow work to accept that living is both stone and fruit, but our poet is here to show us just that.

—Carol Ann Davis,
author of *The Nail in the Tree*

I so admire the zest and precision of Bohm's language and vision—as well as her clear-eyed mistrust of absolutes. While she makes great use of the book's central metaphor, our cartographer host is canny enough to admit early on both that "sometimes maps are not enough" and that "going in circles can still get you there." And while the self she discovers is marked by the people and places she maps and by the act of mapping, Bohm also advises us to: "Sit still / and offer your communion / to disappointment: // open your mouth / like some fat, erotic bird/ and sing." Yes! I was moved and enlivened by this wonderful first collection.

—Ellen Doré Watson, author of *pray me stay eager*

CAREFUL CARTOGRAPHY

Mapping an Autobiography

Poems by
DEVON BOHM

Cornerstone Press
Stevens Point, Wisconsin

Cornerstone Press, Stevens Point, Wisconsin 54481
Copyright © 2021 Devon Bohm
Illustrations © 2021 Maddy Firth
www.uwsp.edu/cornerstone

Printed in the United States of America.

Library of Congress Control Number: 2021944777
ISBN: 978-1-7377390-0-5

Cornerstone Press titles are produced in courses and internships offered by the
Department of English at the University of Wisconsin–Stevens Point.

DIRECTOR & PUBLISHER   EXECUTIVE EDITOR   SENIOR EDITORS
Dr. Ross K. Tangedal   Jeff Snowbarger   Lexie Neeley & Monica Swinick

SENIOR PRESS ASSISTANTS
Claire Hoenecke, Gavrielle McClung

PRESS STAFF
Rosie Acker, CeeJay Auman, Shelby Ballweg, Megan Bittner, Kala Buttke, Caleb Feakes,
Emma Fisher, Camila Freund, Kyra Goedken, Brett Hill, Adam King, Pachia Moua,
Annika Rice, Alexander Soukup, Bethany Webb, Maggie Weiland

For my mother.

All the best parts of me are made of you, and any parts I formed on my own are better for your influence. There are no words but these: thank you.

Contents

HOME

Careful Cartography

The first time I died was in my mother's belly.
They had to scrape me out of her
like they were emptying a cantaloupe
of all that was good to eat.

—

They found me still alive.
They found me screaming.
I splattered my father's glasses with blood
and he fainted,
pitched down hard
to that mess of linoleum
and whatever viscera came with me.

—

I didn't mean to hurt them.
But I am not someone who was born knowing
a word like dishonor
and no matter how many books I devour starving,
I have always spit out that pith, those seeds.

—

I wanted to grow up to be a Cartographer,
but I ended up a writer.
My maps are harder to follow,
and heavier to read,
but they are still trying to lead us somewhere better.

—

Even before I was born, I had to command attention.
I won't pretend to remember,
remembrance is too precious for that, but I can imagine.

I stopped my own heart.

I am the kind of person who will always find a language to suit her.
I have been me, the hollow place for the conversation,
all communications, to echo,
long before my tongue grew in.

———

I studied maps before I learned how to go anywhere.
It has never been about going somewhere.
All of you who crave exquisite, exotic adventure,
I have a secret to tell:

you'll still be there, wherever you go.

This makes all places the same,
and if you're happy, home.

I wasn't born happy.
I was born as I am:
with the careful cartography in my veins aching for home.

———

I have kept dying the way I've kept reading:
like a plough whose furrows hope to be deep enough to seed.
Herbs, flowers without thorns so the bees can make me honey,
can pollinate, so more can blossom, grow.

I am not dying just to get your interest,
I am dying because sometimes maps are not enough.

———

No matter how uncharted the voyage, I have made it this far:
alive and still screaming.

I will never mean to hurt you, but
I have places to be and I have to find a way to speak them.

It is the way I was born.

SAN DIEGO

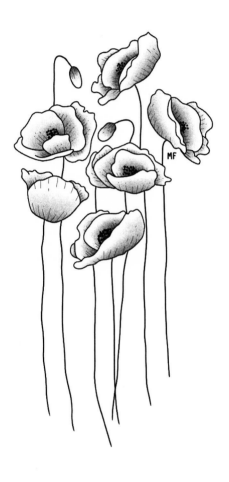

Gardening

I.

Dirt is so many shades   Give me: bole,
sepia, fallow, fawn, sienna   burnt umber
tan, russet, redwood   taupe, buff, ochre, mahogany

I let them fold into me, digging my hands in
little spades
                    I am not gardening, I am burying

I want to make the world grow   but I haven't
          been granted that power

I let the earth crease me, move over me   in waves
But it disallows my tampering, my efforts to change

II.

When I was eight
          my favorite number, the sign for infinity, my birth date
my mother and I moved into a little house
with stone fruit trees   in the backyard
                              apricot and plum
They only bore fruit   that first year
          The leaves like little worms and bruises
                              but no fruit again

The dog dug up our tulip bulbs
                              my favorite flower
then the tiger lilies
then he settled in to eating rocks
                    and mud
and veterinary bills

Then our family killed   the hydrangeas
                    I bought for Mother's Day
Then a desktop bamboo plant
Then
          a cactus

III.
When I was even smaller
                    a rose petal in a palm
we lived in a house somewhere far away   surrounded by citrus
The heavy fruits appeared as if from nothing   year after year
                              we didn't know death yet

My father must have tended them   though I can't remember
              anything but sun, the pool on Christmas

The lemons were so sweet   I ate them sectioned
                                        no sugar
They filled my mouth with sores

I found out years later   I'm allergic
        one of the rarest allergies in the world

I wanted to ask if I'm allergic to dirt too
to growing, if it is really me   who kills everything we try to raise

The pin-prick test   raised welt after welt along my back
But *No*   the technician said   *I'm sorry   We just can't test for that*
His eyes as wet   as a slippery melon half moon

IV.
Twenty years on and
I can't touch the wisteria vine   though I know its climbing
I can only observe a sunflower   from a great distance

A baby robin   a pullet, a colt, a jake died in my yard today
the shell still opening on the pavement   a pale blue
                                        white
speckled, jagged, sharp, a reminder   of what I can do

I have only the power of   a poet
                                    to memorialize
to bury
        and to know: that, too
                        I do poorly

Locust Song

Locusts. Locusts singing in their ten thousand
small voices on the edges of the world. I will always
see you most clearly near these boundaries, near
the water, near the place where you became
a dissolution of the sea. It only takes a fraction
of friction for a cliff to collapse—as a child,
I was never allowed to go into the caves
sawed out of the sandstone, maw open, dark,
waiting for me to join you. Your loss is the cave
I've built my life around, a hole the size and shape
of a bird of paradise. Because grief is both brightly
colored and ugly. I ripped every strelitzia plant
in San Diego up by the roots, I would cry when I saw
the birds' heads growing from the ground. Fifteen
years later, and it's as if I dreamed them. Fifteen years
later and I still look for them as I wind down the cliff
face. I am alone on the trail, midday midweek,
in between where people live life, a tourist on the beach
of my childhood, once my home. There are no
birds of paradise here. Like every other plant
in this desert that falls off into the ocean, they're native
to some other place. Like the locusts. Like me.
Like you sent away to where I cannot see you,
can only know you by the hollow space at the base
of my spine. I name the few plants you taught me:
the Torrey Pines, Ice Plant, the Black-Eyed Susans
I've always envied. I wanted a flower named
after me: *Devon Lily, Devon Rose, Devon Thorn and
Prickle*. Maybe I still envy them, or anything
with such a clear place in the world. The locust song
undulates over the sand, unintentionally straightening out
what I thought I knew, what I thought was hidden
in that gap you left behind: knowing you cannot make
faith where there is only space. But I was wrong.
Space is only more room to build your faith on, so I go in.

To the place I was told could kill me, would kill me,
the place I thought would show me my own face, a bird's
face, speechless and unnamed. It's not as dark
as I'd imagined, nor as shivering. Just a shallow scoop,
a space that's filling in, bursting with the tinny, mechanical
sobs of those just trying to live. On a wall that looks
about to collapse, but I know will keep standing, I carve
For Charlie, and am played out, blinking,
by ten thousand small voices raised to the sun.

Theory on Love: Rocks

I am five
and we are on the beach
and you hold my hand
in your bigger hand,
which swallows mine
like a baseball mitt.

Your body is already at war,
rogue cells are settling satellite colonies
from lung to liver to calf—
but you don't know that yet.

Today, you only know my hand,
your daughter's hand,
as you search for rocks that shift
in salt water, lighting up like spring.

You have willed to your child
your vocation,
a vocation of wanting,
she does not look, but searches,
and it is all you've ever needed:
to know she is your child,
to know she will always be looking.

Later, when you know you're dying,
you will shellac the rocks you collect today
so they will always look wet, transformed,
like something she can hold suspended.

You don't realize it,
but you will be giving her poetry

and knowledge of precisely one thing:

Love isn't just watching someone die,
it's learning how to live again afterward.

Things My Father Taught Me

1. How to make blizzard pancakes—tiny flecks of batter singing in hot grease. That people actually eat and enjoy liver. The best possible meal: sausage links sandwiched between pieces of buttered toast. How to peel back the leaves of an artichoke. The perfection of good, salted popcorn. That cooking a meal—pizza made from scratch on his pizza stone—is a kind of magic. Like making something out of nothing is possible.

2. That extinction is to be avoided at all costs. That season tickets are worth it if you use them right, to the: zoo, aquarium, theme park, lake. How to get suntanned with this pale skin instead of burned. That it's okay to be scared to get wet, climb that playscape meant for the big kids, climb that tree, climb wherever you think might take you somewhere new. Learn something new. That it's good to go out and experience the world.

3. How to bait a hook and swim. That it doesn't matter if you don't catch any fish. Driving a boat is harder than it looks. Whole worlds can be trapped, drowned, unknown under manmade lakes. Don't run near the pool, but if you fall in your father will jump in fully clothed to try to save you. You can save yourself. Regular rocks become something special when you bring them to the water—a little lacquer and you can hold that moment forever. Sometimes only a small piece of forever isn't enough.

4. How to dance—but only on another person's toes. That I'm always going to be too young to watch *The Birds*. Fathers can fall asleep basically anywhere. The best way to fold a shirt. The importance of—and the

word—coordination. That when I'm mad at someone I love, I develop the ability to be aggressively silent. That people who love you will understand when you're aggressively unreasonable. That the people you love will all eventually leave you.

5. The scent of hospitals. What an amputated leg looks like. What stars you can manage to see through windows, radiant emblems you can focus on, even with all the machines beeping. How to trick Mom into giving me cookies. How to say goodbye. What longing is. How unnatural a human being can look before death, the most natural thing of all. The concept of grasping. The idea of grief. The reality of smoking: what really happens when you fill your lungs with that much poison. How others are poisoned too.

6. How saying goodbye is never really a goodbye at all. How writing poems can help you let go. How you don't really want to let go, ever, not ever, when all is said and nothing is to be done. How whatever stage of grief this is, it's two decades too late. How you can miss someone you can barely remember.

The Dead Zone

Nothing is old here, nothing is milk-glass.
All is the bright of a day unfurling
with the luxury of being new.

I swim each morning at dawn,
my body slick as an eel.
La Jolla Cove blossoms red
and phosphorescent,
fish bobbing to the surface.

When I emerge, my eyes have sopped
up the waste and runoff, turning
the clear-jellied pink of placenta
falling heavy from the birth canal.

I look as if I've been crying.
I add my emptiness
to this unfathomable space.

I am young and if I stay here
I will always be young.

The waves here break in sulfur spray,
the oily surface bubbling small and yellow
against a vacant coast, salt leaving
a crusted line in the blackened ash grit.

Up the beach, the dark sand
cradles a jellyfish.
The only one I've ever seen
on my dirty piece
of Southern Californian shore.

I poke it with my toe and it shivers.
Though I would call it dead,
it's truly made of impulse—
those tentacles can still shock,
raise welts that swell
like tautly blown birthday balloons.

Another Word for Dead

Rain. Rain is Poway, California on a famished
Lake I used to fish on with my Father. We
Never caught anything. I ate hard candy until it
Sharpened, made my mouth a wound.
I wished for rain, but it was late.
It came the day you didn't say *I love...*
Anything, certainly not me, but the day you
Formulated us into a sentence, the subject of a
Sentence, our own clause. It came the day we
Nestled into the roots of a tree, tried to wait out
Wetness, tried to revel in it. We could not see how
Deep those roots went, until I was too far
Away to see you anymore. Lightning never
Struck it lengthwise, never broke the tree's pretty,
Wooden heart—the tree is still there, I think.
Remember the fish? When we were walking?
It was the fish I had never caught, it
Climbed up the land in search of my hook and
Died there. It lay just under the bridge, over
Nothing, near where the waterfall used to be, wasn't
Anymore, mica glinted where water used to
Breathe. The scales didn't snag on the disappearing
Light, the storm rushed in, it was as dull as all
Dead Things are because it was dead. When the
Rain came I hoped for something for the first time since
My Father, But. But a sudden California storm is
Vicious. It rendered the softening fish belly and when
We were soaked through we went to the car.
When we were through in the car, the sun was out
Again, and the fish, the fish was still dead.
My mouth raw with yours, it still felt like a
Wound. The tree stood silent, shaken of its
Leaves. I never asked for anything again.

What I'm Thinking While You're Talking

1. You don't love me.

2. You wouldn't know how to love me,
even if I wrote you a list,
step by step.

3. If I really had been pregnant,
that embryo would have been
half someone who can't be bent
into loving.

4. If I had to guess, I would say
this color of sky is cerulean, those clouds
nimbus, and my foot asleep.

5. Saying you love everything is barren,
limp. It's the same as saying you love
nothing. You can't value everything
at exactly the same worth. Then everything
is worth nothing because value is meaningless
when everything is equal.

6. What kind of man cuts his crusts off
his sandwiches? It has all the vitamins,
the nutrition, my mother used to tell me
it would make your hair curl, it's the best
part.

7. I didn't know violets
could bloom so late
in the summer.
Global warming,
spasms of growth.

8. People can't survive in a standstill.
Even bereaving something would be
a kind of movement, even the world
warming is some kind of change.

9. The mosquitoes are biting, swarming,
gorging their tiny stomachs
on the richness of my blood.
They like the way I taste.
They like what's inside of me.

10. The world looks scooped out
in this much sun—a bowl
we sit in the center of. We can't
climb up these sloped sides.

11. What if it's too late now,
what if we're stuck with each other?

12. I'd imagine it's tiring, too.
To be springing endlessly forward.

13. With your hair matted down
from sleep, it looks like
a bear pelt. You look like
you could rend me without teeth.

14. I think that's what you're doing.

15. You don't love me.

16. Everything is tiring.

17. Everything isn't worth loving.

18. I am. I am. I am.

Coriolis Effect

Your heart seized. Rolled over. Died.
I woke up knowing what disaster means,
how to call a warning through the black
pitch and tumble of moving through the
night. I love you, wait. Please come back.

I have never broken a bone. But in
this changing air the scent of skin burns
and in it I imagine the cracked
and jagged scrum of my bones meeting
the ground. I can feel this earthquake,
full of quivers and shivering faults.

Bodies as deep as Earth flailing against
gravity, the bait and switch of magnetic
poles, but we are never safe from this—
a shift. A swirl of land that doesn't know
how to do anything but surprise. To open
itself and bleed out in a storm, or not.

You were named after a hurricane,
to flesh out natural disaster, to fear
the results. I can call you a volcano.
I can make you a tsunami. A flash flood.
A seismic boom of too many people
in the kitchen, banging plates together.
Yet I am a woman who has never broken

a bone.

The C-Word

My father doesn't have a grave
which doesn't mean anything for anyone
except my mother,
who's never had anything to cry over.

I have this aunt, my mother's sister,
who refuses to say certain words too loudly.
For the longest time I only knew
cancer as a whisper.

We don't choose our family
and we can't choose our death,
but I know
if I were my mother
I'd slap her
and scream all that illness
into the air.

Forgiveness

In the two years between my father's death, his lung cancer, and your
almost-loss, your heart attack, I began to see signs, beacons silvering
the dark: white cigarette papers, white paleness of fingers, white coats,
white eggshells in the white sink with no eggs to show for them,
white sweeter than its own sugar, that white of a mild oblivion.
You think you're owed my forgiveness because you're my mother,
now, but what about then? Rule #1: All poets are monsters.
Your grief made you a poet. Your grief made one of me too.
I became a poet the day you made me limp back into the metallic-
scented dusk of the hospital to see another parent spread out
across the whiteness of sheets like a stain. Nicotine-yellow, an old
bruise come to meet me. I began a habit then I'll never shed,
I name people by the way I think they'll leave me: in death,
by accident, of their own volition, selfishly, selfishly, selfishly.
Rule #2: All poets are optimists. In these past two decades
we have become geniuses of the distracted barb, of inflicting pain
on the most tender swath of flesh, we have checked in together
to the hospice of living with each other. We have never walked
on the same sand again, and though you have never smoked another
cigarette, my name for you is still White Smoke. I still see it hanging
above your head, a brain-fire, misfire, wetting the white hairs
at your scalp as if with dew. If I was fair, I'd throw stones at my
father's ghost as well. But what joy can one grasp in yelling at the dead?
Rule #3: All poets are sadists. It's the same amount of joy I hold
when I dog about after you. I'd like to think I could never
make my mother cry, but if I'm being honest we wring each other
out with each crack of the neck, each blink, each twist of hair
and each eyeballed moment. If I'm being honest, some part of me
wants to, wants you to feel like I do. Rule #4: All poets are masochists.
The skin on the backs of your hands is shivery, paper husked
in half, gutted—those veins trace a history of waving pain away,
of gathering it back to us again. They are blue, purple, they
are bruises, they are shadows of the same bird wings etched beneath

my sleeping eyelids, the ones that wake me. I know that. I know
it all, but. But isn't my inability to forgive you a kind of love?
You mean too much to me. I have kept you only a breath away,
an exhalation, a smoke away from me for all these long, broken years.
I would never show this poem to anyone, I promise. I would
never tell what I can still feel you doing to me: forgetting, leaving,
so selfishly, selfishly, selfishly. Remember. Rule #5: All poets are liars.

The Truth of Birth

We all die alone,
what they say is true.

But we arrive on earth
attached to another,
alone only after skin is severed,
only after the wail spins off into—

I was born in the afternoon
after three days of labor.
My heart stopped in the womb.

If I died then,
I would never have had the same fate
as the rest of humanity:
to die without my mother,
but worse,
to hurt her.

The truth of birth is harder than death:
no matter how you deliver,
more than a child comes out of it.

You gain a wound.

Things My Mother Taught Me

If you're uninterested in the world, it's because you're uninteresting. Don't let a man serenade you. A little salt goes a long way. Most clothes are better off air drying. An accent rug is a great way to bring a room together. No one is a stranger, we're all just people—half-strangers only. Plan your grocery list by the route you take through the supermarket. When it rains it inevitably downpours, bring an umbrella. Funerals aren't for the dead. Don't love a man who drinks gin. If you keep eating that much salt, you're going to develop high blood pressure. You wouldn't get so many headaches if you drank more water. 3 a.m. is both too late and too early for your bullshit. You don't need two parents, even if it would have been nice. Any hurricane can be weathered if you can find a safe harbor, if you move far enough inland. Any fire can be survived if you make your way toward the coast. You can build a palace wherever you land. Don't go near the edge of the cliffs—erosion. Don't fuck with snakes, just get out of there. Or wasps. Most people would be better off without tombstones. If your spouse dies, you become a wonder of the world if you can manage to keep going. Taste before you season. Yawning when someone else does is a sign of natural empathy. It's okay to ask for what you want. Always have wine in the house. If you pretend to be happy, the pretending will become real, eventually. Expiration dates are meaningless. Life is relentless, so you'll have to be relentless, too. Love isn't the kind of thing that dies when a person dies. Red is a little much for a bedroom, maybe try the kitchen. It costs nothing to be kind, but you wouldn't know it from other people. Unconditional love is the only option when you really care. Devon, that is definitely too much salt. It's illegal to have the car's inside light on at night. (It's not.) You have one job in this life: Be better. Be kinder. Be more than those that came before you. Eat when you're hungry and listen to your body to tell you when it's full. Unconditional love is worth whatever pain comes with it. When you're lost, go back to the ocean. Anything and anyone can be holy. Even with that much salt.

Map of San Diego

Torrey Pines: The State Park: 1989

I scraped my knuckles trying to climb free
of the Miner's Tub, left a wreath of blood
around the bath of men who must have been giants,
carved and corroded and cracked their imprints
into the rock on the beach, all twisted pine and crust of salt.

The hang gliders from the cliffs above
dipped and swam above my bloody hands,
sizzling their way through the cloudburst, astounding the flowers—
pink anemones so full of the sea they refused to burn.

I was illiterate and cold and only flesh as flesh is meant to be—
exposed.

Carmel Mountain: The Suburbs: 1996

If you were lucky, they would let you plant an orange tree
and the heavy globes of juice would pop
from the branches and roll lazy into the street.

The trees would swell but the fruit was always blowsy and dull,
scarred and unwaxed—nothing like the supermarket.

They would make dunes in the road of their pulpy little bodies—
weaponized and tart, more yellow than orange,
we didn't run after them.

We were addicts of the collision, of the statement made
when that faint spray would release itself from the rind,
tint the air with citrus and a sound like a bird falling to earth.

Julian: The Mountains: 2005

I didn't know for sixteen years that it could snow this
far south.

You stole me away into the mountains,
introduced me to this marble vault of cold

with my mouth held open for apple pie and fried pickles,
egg creams and the same acorn paste as two hundred years ago.

I was full, you filled me, brought me to an antique store
so we could remember things we hadn't yet lost:
headless dolls, sepia photographs of the dead,
thousands of matchbooks, a cameo brooch, a pram,
a deer's head stuffed and mounted, one glove, a trunk, a ring—

your hands with dust caught and whispering in the cracks.

Downtown: The City: 2008

It doesn't rain here, so the streets can't shine.

Even with all these lights—neon blaring bright and belling out
into the dark—there's something small about this city,
the way all those efforts black out the stars.

There is only one absolute:
the loamy, sewer smell like lumps of vegetation left and rotting,
needling its way through the crowds.

Del Mar: The Beach: Someday

El Niño is unpredictable,
gives a stormless place its share of water
reaching out to swallow the shore, the houses, the dogs
on their doggy beach near the salt marshes and the bridge.

The surfers caw in joy
as the tide echoes and resounds,
taking black tar mouthfuls of the sand—
all that ash left over from each November's fires.

There won't be fires this year, only a mirage of weather,
a wafer on the dry, parched tongue of the earth.

I won't be there to see it.

I'll have to imagine it.

INTERLUDE: LONDON

Learning to Love in Camden

I learned to love you in Camden Town, not because you were hard to love,
but because I just didn't know how yet. I learned to love you in that year there,

a school year, nine months, the gestation it takes to create a whole new person
in London's tube zone 2 and beyond. I learned to love you from behind the counter

of the coffee shop next to the black watered lock and its incongruous kayakers,
its Dutch levy. I learned to love you on the bridge over the lock that was kissed

by the branches of a willow, that led to the used bookstore where you bought me
The Unbearable Lightness of Being and the stained-glass windows made you feel

like you were breathing underwater. I learned to love you in the Stables Market
with the vendors selling: silk-screened shirts, fur coats made from unborn lambs—

a black, nubby wool—guides for palmistry, thousands of old teacups and saucers,
maps and luggage and CDs and mulled wine. I learned to love you in the greasy café

just before Regent's Park with its cold toast and gray coffee and crusted ketchup
bottles in the shapes of tomatoes on red-and-white checkered plastic. I learned

to love you in Queen Mary's Garden, where they set up little plaques to name
the roses: Sexy Rexy, Deep Secret, Ingrid Bergman, Singin' in the Rain, Invincible,

Especially For You. I learned to love you on Primrose Hill for Guy Fawkes Night,
drinking straight from a bottle so high up we could see every firework and bonfire

in London. I learned to love you walking back to my flat at 3 a.m., sweaty and soaked
from the rain and KOKO nightclub, when you smiled at the homeless man who always

wore cut-offs and had a lilac balloon and waved at the tall red buses unzipping
the streets. I learned to love you in The Lock Tavern, The Electric Ballroom, Proud

Camden, The Hawley Arms, The World's End pub just outside the tube stop
with its Irish folk band and Strongbow cheap and bad toasties and a man always

at the end of the bar, drinking alone, dressed as a pirate. I learned to love you
in my dingy bedroom, in my bed, the one built into the wall under a picture window

with no screen that let in pigeons and every ounce of sunlight the cloudy city
had to offer past the bottles collecting on the sill. I learned to love you in the heat

of that window, sleeping naked into mid-morning, skin stuck to skin after the first
time we loved, after all the times later in my bed made for one. I learned to love you

even when the nine months went by and I was a new person and the plane came
and the landscape changed. I learned. I loved you. I never wanted to learn again.

Anomalies of the Natural World

You know, like volcanoes.
The platypus. Electric storms.
Sinkholes. Asteroids. Jupiter's
lost stripe. Water that flows
uphill. The blue people
of Kentucky. Conjoined twins
sharing one heart. Fire.
The half ounce weight
of a soul. That actress
with the lips. Spring.
Clouds. Back dimples. Red
algae lakes. Red hair.
Spontaneous human combustion.
Striped icebergs. Double
rainbows. The wide, wide
Sargasso Sea. White ravens.
Cancer. That kiss three
Novembers ago. Migrating
desert stones. Hypnosis.
Words. Communication.
Language. Poetry. You.
The way your body
generates heat in your
sleep, a spot of thunder
baldness. Dancing with me
in the kitchen to no music,
bare feet a brush fire on
kitchen tile. Your ear to me
across distance, time. A
heartbeat in stillness, a small,
tiny punch I feel in my ribs.
The cryptozoological miracle
of your hands. The indefinable
thing that happens in the
millimeter of space between us,
between breaths. Our love that
undulates like a jellyfish—
our creature without brain or teeth.

Three Scenes, No Metaphors

1.
Why do light bulbs burn out? I'd look it up, but that
would take all the story out of it. Think about the light
bulb: it's nothing on its own, it's an un-light bulb, it's a
conduit only. You keep pouring that much energy into
anything and one day, eventually, finally—anything would
make a sound like breaking. Anything would reach a
point where anything just can't take it anymore. This is
no eureka moment. I have found exactly nothing. This
isn't a parable. This is what I was thinking the last time I
saw you.

2.
That last hot asphalt day I was asserting your name
against my tongue, first and last pressed together as one
word, like a kiss. The wreck was behind us. A man on
a motorcycle spun out and skidded and slid across the
black tar pavement, stopped. The sound was silence, but
louder, and we couldn't help but rubberneck, unstick our
foreheads from each other to stare. He stood and walked
to us—the crash had ripped his shirt open and the smell
of his skin made me hungry before you could open your
mouth. This is not a metaphor. This is just the way it
happened. Maybe. As best as I can tell.

3.
I don't know the names of any birds, but if you were a
bird, you'd be that one. From here he's only a black speck
forcing the horizon to rise around him, but I can tell he's
graceful. I can tell how natural it is for him to wheel off
and away from here, lifted by the air running over under
the curve of his wings. I can tell he knows how to move in
a direction away from entropy. I can tell he wouldn't know
either, how to say such an immense goodbye, the kind of
goodbye that really isn't goodbye at all.

Grocery Shopping With You

was as exciting as museums, the way you looked in museums
like the Tate Modern when we lived in London and I was
catapulted into you—it was ruthless, an oven-fresh kind of love
that sprang out of the way you looked at things, as if they were
oranges and you were sucking out the pith of them or maybe
the way you moved through that one display, that stuttering
lapse in judgment that was the giant-sized table and chairs
hanging above your head because those misfits were so big you
walked under them your palms not touching, but skirting so
lightly, looking but not touching and bringing them

new life by the way you gave them something less myopic than
a human eye, as if you were tall enough to see the tops

or maybe as good as going to Marseille, which we chose
because they mention the city in *Casablanca*, the sea-town
foaming up, snoring away in sleep with salted ticks against
time passing when we took the little boat to the Ile d'If, that
island prison unchanged from the days it housed a guard
rhinoceros and *The Count of Monte Cristo* and was stained with
its wallowing, a clamshell beach that was lapped by water not
emerald or turquoise, but a gray you made gather its sheen to
throw on my hair, bees droning lazily in black-eyed Susans as
you took my picture and told me you loved the way I stood
solo, alone, apart, and my mouth looked like I had been eating
blueberries so raw it was from kissing you

and even later, after you were not mine, after we were not each
other's for reasons, reasons were given but still, still

even later when I visited you in your new-old home in
Chicago and we saw the Bean, but you did not look closely
or take pictures because you passed it every day on your way
to work, you suggested we go to the store for milk and bread
and everything bagels, but you stopped yourself, knowing
such a trip would be too intimate, too much like sex, more
like sex than the sex we had that morning in your new-old
bed, pretending we no longer loved, were no longer lovers,
pretending intimacy, that picking out ripe avocados, was the
dirtiest act of all

Growing Ghosts

1.
I live here. Here, among the intricate folds and bows of the ghost orchid.
I don't mean Cuba, or Florida, but that I appear to float from the trunk

of the Cypress tree—that I am my own symbol of mourning. That I don't
understand photosynthesis, that I don't have leaves. That I am nearly impossible

to propagate, that I need such specific conditions to grow: a giant sphinx moth,
sphagnum moss, someone to look for me. That for nearly 20 years, no one

thought to think I existed. But I do. I live here, a specter in the heavy air.
I live here, waiting for someone to remember me.

2.
You would find me ungrateful, if we still spoke.

Or if not ungrateful, at least exhausted

by the enormity of the self you made me see.
I took you to *Macbeth* in London,

murder most foul in the open air,

the indelible poetry of the Old Globe.
We stood in the yard, good townsfolk, peasants—

the unique, cold experience of a master's work on his own stage.

You were quiet, holding me from behind,
until the first lines unfurled in witch-shrieks,

When shall we meet again? / In thunder, lightning, or in rain?

and the storm broke open, veiling us from the stage.
But I could see clearly the way you saw me:

you knew I called the thunder down.

And I was Atlas in that moment.
I was holding up the heavens in my arms

as Lady Macbeth's nightgown drifted, a floating orchid, alone.

As she bloodied the already wet stage.

3.
I've never been inside a hothouse, but I imagine them a prison.
Mausoleums fattened with lushness and mold scent, wheezing

out stagnant life. But perhaps I'm jealous: I have killed everything
I've tried to get to grow beside me. I am only one flower on one type

of moss pollinated by one type of moth grown on one type of tree,
and I have seen all of them leave me. I am rare, but I'm not sure rare

actually means special. I want to write: everyone you've ever loved
lives inside you. I want to write: I remember me, I find myself, I am
enough.

But the incandescent rind of green around my frills can't lie:
it could be 20 years before someone sees me again, before

I am made to see myself. Now that you're gone I am deep in the wild,
having burned every pane of green glass in effigy. I am beautiful and

I am lonely and I want the weight of another again,
even if it crushes the last ghost orchid in all the world.

The Face of God

1.
The way I see it, the Tower of Babel was probably just a ladder
and an idea: *I want to see the face of God*. But God doesn't seem
to like anyone questioning his wounding. That's all I learned,
reading the bible during the few years I insisted on trying the
church thing out. I wanted to understand the shape of the cross,
how the triangle of the trinity fit in, all those hawkish corners
and sharp edges making up grace. Instead, I spent the time
ignoring the mottled syllables pouring off the altar to read the
Old Testament again and again. I liked Old Testament God.
He seemed more likely. He seemed prepared for my insolence.
The church liked to do baptisms in the estuary—they called it
a godly place, that space between salt and fresh, land and sea—
the California wetlands are all sanctuary, by law. I stayed home
the day it was my turn. I never looked back, not even idly. But
I've never considered any decisions I've made final.

2.
Look around: what some people call miracles, I call deceptions.
Like today in the news, I read a study that tried to console
me by telling my sleeplessness: don't worry, in one out of four
people, scientists found they could *produce* memory. Meaning,
not produce memory, but trick the brain into believing it could
remember things that never happened. My mother used to say,
The human brain is a miracle, as if she knew something about it.
For years I've wondered if the way she mourned over my father
could be real. Now I know: maybe not. Maybe she's mourning
something she made up. Maybe I'm mourning someone she
made up for me, implanted. Maybe he was awful. Me, I try not
to play around with memory. I just try to forget.

3.
If God made this world, he filled it with people with faces like
Rorschach blots—we only see something of ourselves in each
other. Why wouldn't we want to see the face of God? I want
to know if it's the same: a collection of keyholes and bananas,
of bats and axes, of human faces and bodies, pieces and parts
doubled and mirrored, dancing, falling in love. In high school, I
told my therapist this. She asked me about my father and told
me God was my stand in for a male role model. She predicted I

would always have problems with men, that I would always be
looking for someone to answer my questions. I told her I didn't
believe in God. She said, Exactly. As if this confirmed me. She
never held any inkblots up, just gave me a test that asked me
how much I agreed with statements. *I like gardening magazines,
the color green, the voices in my head, being outside, laughing, etc.
etc. etc. Strongly agree, agree, not sure, disagree, strongly disagree.*
I answered everything *not sure* because I wasn't sure. About
anything, but especially about absolutes.

4.
If I had a ladder and any belief I know what I'd ask that sleepy
face, bored with all the inquiries: why would you give me a man
with hands like water and a mind like a sun cleaved in half,
always rising, always setting, and a face I could see a person in,
why would you give me a man like that if I wasn't allowed to
keep him? Or: was he real? Was waking up to strong coffee in a
mug with a bear real, his knuckles white rapids when he held it
out to me, the way his wrists cracked? Was dancing barefoot to
records on Sunday afternoons real, my back eventually pressed
up against the wall with his maps from canoeing trips, the way
we'd make lists of all the small things for each other, whispered
in the places between songs? Was the moth he wouldn't kill in
the dorm room in London real, was the desire real, the more
than desire real, is it real now? Or: is the present memory, too?
Is what I've become maybe only a trick of the light, the fasting,
the spasming cry, the beaten feeling that refuses to go back
to sleep in my chest? Should I be worried I made him up and
that I feel like this for no reason? Could I really have imagined
a face like that, a man like that? Could I really have imagined
seeing for the first time?

Or: could he come back?

5.
For all my climbing, I know what I can't know: that mess of
crabs and balloons would remain inscrutable, would only scatter
my alphabet to the wind. I would never be able to articulate the
answer God's face gave me: I don't know. Not sure. *I don't know.*

Things London Taught Me

That sometimes courage is getting on a plane by yourself
to go live in a city where you know exactly no one. How
to drink beer. You can get cheap tickets for anything in
the West End if you show up 5 minutes before curtain.
That headphones don't even have to be on to help you
avoid catcallers. English people don't seem hostile, but
they tend to eat cold toast. Not how to navigate, but
patience for when I inevitably get lost. How much I can
love.

That you can be held hostage by your own self-pity—
you won't see it until you let it all go. How and where
to get a black cab. The routes of all the night buses.
The word *flaneur*. How to be a flaneur: how to push
through the chaos of a city without a destination in
mind. That flesh can ache in a good way, too. That
going in circles can still get you there. That some shoes
aren't up for it, but many boots can be resoled. If you don't
speak, people will assume you're French or Spanish—
let them.

That forgetting who you were made into is the best way
to become yourself. No one uses the word "loo." Any pub
with the word "harp" in the name is probably okay. Going
and getting a job and feeding yourself is enough to make you
feel like an adult. My proper coffee preference: white Americano.
My drink preference: anything without citrus, really, a Snakebite
will do. That you can be enthralled equally by a person and a
place.

How quickly you miss green. How green a city can be if you
just look for it—the aria of clematis vines climbing the boughs
of the new trees in Regent's, Kensington, Hyde Park. That I
could tremble at a touch, that I could want to be that vulnerable.
That Sherlock Holmes's address never existed, that Shakespeare's
Globe is a rebuilt approximation, that Sylvia Plath doesn't get
a historical blue plaque where she died because she was American—
heartbreaking.

That you can't be homesick when you don't know where home is anymore. That you can still miss a country you aren't particularly proud to belong to. That you could miss things as simple as popcorn and peanut butter. How to ignore the bloody wail of sirens and fire alarms when you need to sleep. The irony of all the forces in the world bringing me to you, at least for a little while. What the word irony feels like when it's dramatic: that maybe everyone else can see what you're failing to, over and over again. My own capacity for loneliness, but also love.

All years come to an end, eventually. How to do latte art. Sometimes, things can be beautiful enough to forgo suffering, at least for a little while. How to eat mayonnaise. How to get the most out of what I paid for. That we create home inside ourselves, but sometimes the person we hope might have the key to the front door doesn't know what we're talking about. How love is like that. How much I love trains.

That sometimes courage is going back, especially when you don't want to. That geography can only pretend to change you. That people are the same, no matter where you go, as places are: they'll leave you or you'll leave them. How to cry. That we keep going.

Impossible Ceiling

Start by doing what's necessary; then do what's possible;
and suddenly you are doing the impossible.
—St. Francis of Assisi

My mother didn't raise me with religion
but she grew up Catholic
with her mother a devotee
of St. Francis of Assisi.

Named two of her children after him—
a boy and a girl—
that generous man, always
helping animals, the sick.

Saintly things,
things I don't really know anything about.

I wasn't raised to be anything but
strong, and if today I could go back
to St. Francis's church with its impossible
ceiling and pay a dollar for a small,
white candle, I would.

I would pray for the woman
I was meant to be.

I would pray she still has the wherewithal
to last all this out.

My Advice

I've heard you're disappointed with the world.
I know the feeling.

When the world changes,
it changes quickly.
Happiness bursts in, a sudden squall,
and bursts out again to leave you
dry and baking
and cracked along the edges.

So you go to the sea,
maybe all the way to California.
The people are bronze,
the sand is bronze,
but there is water.

A briny womb cradles you,
lifts you on the crest of a purple wave,
lifts you toward the mountains,
peeks over palm trees to open desert.

This isn't one world, but two, three—
landscapes on top of landscapes,
colliding with you in between,
blood-roses bursting on your thighs.

There is too little and too much—
their disappointments are equal
and equally full, both snapping
at your heels as you run
to another shore, dune-specked,
another ocean with a simpler coastline.

My advice?

Sit still
and let your disappointment
wash over you.

Sit still
and offer your communion
to disappointment:

open up your mouth
like some fat, erotic bird
and sing.

New England

What We Shouldn't Discuss in Poems
The Poet Talks to Herself

You make a beautiful table arrangement
of forsythia and oranges—because it's spring
and you're from California and homesick
in all this rain. You use words like "beautiful"
because you know they don't mean anything.
Not like Beauty. You have forgotten how to speak
with such capitalization. You have forgotten
so many things.

You like to take walks in the woods.
There were no trees like this in California,
no clarity of green. In all that quiet, you
become enthralled with your own heart,
its constant stops and starts, undressed
for you and slick. But the truth is, you
have a pathetic little heart.
I don't say this to be cruel,
but because you need to remember:
You have the heart of some extinct species
that fed only on longing, chaos, all the things
we pretend are unnatural. You've been ravaged
too many times.

You have so many bad dreams.
You can't remember those either,
so you go back to sleep only to wake up again
sweating, not sure if you're breathing,
not sure that you're you. You live in a circle.
You are trying to wed ignorance and living,
but you can't. You can't put all the things
you will away into dreams.
The dream can't rescue the dreamer,
because only the dreamer is real.
Those tears are real. Your small,
sad heart is real.

You can see yourself grieving.
You just wish you remembered
what you were grieving for.

Winter is Coming

Are those ravens or rooks
giving rout to the southwest?

It doesn't matter.

A blackbird is a blackbird is a blackbird,
even when it's not.

—

I wasn't ready for this—
black on white on nothing.

A world where cold grows
as if one snowflake is a seed and two,
well, they rubbed their backs against each other
and I am here, thigh-sunk in cloudbank all wet wool
and no such thing as floating.

I could rust here, a heartless woman,
a wood's ghost scaring bears away
with all my wishes of Africa,
my hypothermic thoughts:

Consider the electric eel, children.
How beautiful would it be to make your own heat?

—

This lead sky is no aperture,
but a ceiling.

God isn't watching me shiver,
isn't weighing me on a scale
as my under hue shifts from pink to blue,

no—I am alone here.

—

Even the snowman is silent,
though his face is ecstatic.
Not real, not real,
just the thumbprint inside my eyelids
of some long-forgotten cartoon.

—

I was never a survivor,
never the woman
with a spear in one hand
and lipstick in the other,
never much for that blood red pigment at all.

No, come to think of it,
who needs peacocks?

In this colorless world
it will be so much easier to sleep and sleep and sleep—

—

No, my strange bird,
my indefinable bird,
keep flying.

Keep flying until you reach a place
where your feathers won't freeze
to your shriveled, starveling chest.

Because the Snow Comes Every Year

The first time I saw crocuses I was eighteen and I wanted
to die. What can I say? With awareness like knives I knew
I was done—the world had stopped wooing me long ago.
That winter was my first winter, it embalmed me in cold,
the way winters can do, it made me too sad to see the leaves
still an unreal orange against the bleach of the snow, against
the black rasp of bark. But sad isn't the word for it, no,
it made me lyrical. It made me lyrical to see the season
cartwheel right over me. It made me a poem, it made me a song,
it made me something not long for the world. So it became
my habit to take long walks in the woods by the school,
dreaming of blackbirds I never saw in the trees, blackbirds
like small, dark angels, blackbirds like ill-fashioned brides.
I was waiting for spring to come, waiting for what I thought
would be a 100 Year Flood of the Mill River, waiting for Paradise
Pond to thaw out, waiting for the girls to stop skating over
the filthy ice, their bodies knocking the world together when
they fell, kissing, their cheeks like the blush of summer peaches.
I was waiting for the soil to turn over, to reveal the small aspirins
of seeds and old cigarette butts, waiting for the infamous snails
to be risen with their acidic little bodies ascending my arms
and legs as if I were mountains, slowly, slowly, waiting for
the pinecones to peel back their scales to show their tiny meats.
I was waiting for pale pink flowers opening through the sky
like clouds, rinsed clean by the kindness of the air, gluing
freshness to my shoulder blades and collarbone, waiting to find
petals inside my clothing, wetted and damp, floating off
my breasts in the tub water. I was waiting for a climax,
I was waiting for proof. I was waiting for conclusive proof
because I thought I was too smart to take the world at its word.

I was waiting for something to stop me.

And then: the usual miracle. Usual miracles are something minor
and delicate, something hidden on the surface, something forsaken,

by people not looking for deliverance. An April storm had broken me across its knees—I couldn't fend off my lyricism any longer.

I took a walk and there, rocketing upward from their basket of fresh snow, sprang blooms belling up into the dry, drained air. Pale lilac, close to white, close to the color of my bruised, sleepless eyelids: crocuses, a flower I had only read about in books. I'm not saying crocuses saved my life, don't be ridiculous, I'm saying I did.

I'm saying if I can do it once, I can do it again. I'm saying I can find conclusive proof somewhere out there to round off, to ward off, to pay the toll of whatever lyricism I might, maybe sometimes, feel. And that I need to remember: only time can give me that.

Things I Learned By Staying Alive

Sometimes, just making it through
another day is an accomplishment.

—

Horseshoe crabs look like prehistoric beasts.
How to go clamming. That letting go is the only
way to move forward. You can claim your own
heart first. The weirdest people make the best
friends—they understand. How to read a star map.
How to appreciate abstract art, even as the crabs
draw it, even as it's effaced by the unceasing waves.

—

That you can write. That other people will want to read it.
That it can save you. That you can save yourself.

—

My favorite type of latte: lavender. The language
of flowers. For renewal, you'll need both dirt and
shit. How deep to plant a seed. That thinking of
the future can be terrifying, but that it won't not
happen because you hoped for it. It's okay to hope
for things. How long to steep a tea bag—green for
less time than black. How to make a flower crown.

—

That most people in America live past eighty now—
you have so much time left to achieve whatever you want
to do with your life. That achieving things doesn't matter
unless you're happy. That real happiness won't come
from those achievements. Real happiness lives inside you.

—

How much I love weddings. That maybe, maybe I want
to get married someday. That the word "sinner" is very
objective. That I don't like New York, but I do like

Seattle and London. How to fold a fitted sheet. How to deglaze a pan and why. What true passion is, and also, more importantly, how much better it is when paired with real affection. That maybe, maybe I want kids.

—

That it's okay to be scared of the world.
That it's okay to be excited about the world.
That it's okay to care about the world.

—

How to crate-train a dog. That no matter how many red and gold sunrises you see over the Sound, there will be another tomorrow. How to comfort a quivering dog during a firework show. Don't you want to see another? How to be comforting, to yourself and to others. That you do want to see another. And another.

—

That direct articulation of the gray room that is depression will always fall short of its obliterating weight. That it's easier to define it by what it's not. That it's a monster. To remember: you can save yourself.

—

To remember: just making it through another day is always enough.

Bunker Hill Monument: Some Spring

I know your view is the top of my head.
Where the baby hairs take wing
toward your hungry storm of a mouth.

—

The sun edges its way to the spring
furling from the hollows of you—
bones breaking their way to the surface
through the cupped, honeyed light.

The dog approaches the bed,
whines new longing into a room
where everything is full.

—

Outside, the frost-fingered chill
is transparent, fading toward the heat
we left in the attic bedroom,
sun clawing through the skylight yawning up—
open to some disapproving Godhead.

But how could anyone not watch
the pulse between us,
see the silence at our center,
and not say *Yes?*

Even the dog turns back to look.

—

The Bunker Hill Monument
is silk in the new morning,
then again stone, spiking toward heaven
but unable to shake the moss from its base.

There is a famine in your eyes.
You want to be that tall.

—

The trees are cotton wool.
I want to spin it out between a skein
of two trees that release a scent
like your sweat and skin,
cover you in a sweater.

Catch my nail and let a line of red
shoot through the fabric,
so you know my love is in it.

I want to keep standing here,
in a day laced with what's possible.

———

Summer will come, crash
in all electric lightning static,
a frozen flower in the sky,
a mirror, a reflection, a window.

I will watch you wilt.
I will love it all.

I will eat each moment and be hungry for more.

The Shame of Forgetting

That summer came wet to New England,
filling her with unquiet—the restlessness
of the never quite dry, flower heads bowing
under the heft of the damp.

Amidst the gray tickling the errant ends
of my hair You painted the kitchen—
You called it yellow, I called it atrocious,
You threw things, I cried.

I said, *I remember when there was blue,*
and You hid your face with the shame
of forgetting.

There was nothing left to do but keep
a glass jar of blue on the counter,
between the little, hard brains of walnuts
and the snow dust of flour.

Nothing left but to watch the water-logged
world teeming with life, storming through
August.

Nothing left but the carnal surge in my abdomen
each time I stood at the counter
alone, eating berries,
the juices running down my face.

Learning to Love in Connecticut

Five years since we last spoke
and I can finally admit to myself:
you were my intentional scar.
A seedling buried too deep, and watered
too heavily, a campfire left to burn
the whole forest down, the bite marks
on my hands made by my own teeth.
It has taken half a decade for me
to write down what I had always
known: you were mine only
for a little while, I was never
going to marry you, that even as I
felt baptized by the pure force
of your love, it would one day
drain away. I knew. I knew, but yet
the knife-blade of your leaving
was body temperature and I didn't
feel it slide in—only the bleeding,
bleeding for years trying to learn how
to trust empty hands again, how
to trust full words again, how
to know that the entire alphabet
in any combination couldn't give
me what only I had the power
to give myself: I never expected
to keep you. I was just scared
no one would ever love me like
you could again. Five years since
we last spoke and I am learning
that I hadn't seen anything yet.

Things I Do Instead of Believing in You

Listen (!) to the white noise of New England. Drink
vodka out of a solo cup on the rocky, sharp beach. Look
for shapes in clouds and find a double-headed axe.
Read volumes of poetry that make my hair twist and
curl. Bake cakes I can never eat. (Somehow allergic to
lemons.) Open the basement boxes when I forget what's
inside. Swim for hours, refuse to come in when called
to shore. Draw sketches that never become, just fall into
abstraction. Eat yellow tomatoes and yellow cherries and
asparagus. Swing on the porch with legs akimbo, kicking
up all air. Watch dragonflies dip and tumble in the sky,
two attached. Sleep accidentally in a field of clover
flowers, make crowns. Paint my nails, boxes, canvases, just
one side of the house. Stand between the gravestones of
people I never knew. Take pictures, only to delete them
all later, when alone. Coast down a hill, almost crash, have
a graceful recovery. Pretend to be thirteen instead of my
distinguished twenty-three. Lie when I meet strangers
in sticky, sweaty bar rooms. Tell stories to small children
about lightning and coyotes. Stay up all night, not doing
anything, no escapades but being. Look at the stars from
the lifeguard stand at three a.m. Realize how little I know
of the world beyond my books. Hold hands with a friend
when I'm happy, not just sad. Cry over fictional characters
and all those squished bugs. Light bonfires with a flint,
such a good little girl scout. Write poems in the quietest
ache of a new morning opening. Let my hair grow out,
ragged ends touching fingertips. Cut off that ex-boyfriend
who broke me over his knee. Study for tests that don't test
anything, preliminary to nothing. Make myself get out of
bed so I can do something, anything. Kiss you, learning
to forget whoever you are, already gone. Learn that all the
white noise is cicadas, rubbing their legs together, going
nowhere, but believing in the possibility of flight.

Northern Lights

I was born searching for a green sky,
always waiting on a seam to split open
and reveal beautiful, impossible things.

When summer lights the world,
puts off the dark throat of night a little longer,
it's easy to believe.

It's easy to dance to the wild symphony
that is belief without proof.

My beliefs aren't hard to explain,
all the spinning stops on one fugitive thought:
you.

I believe you're coming back,
even though I saw what fire made of you.

I expected blood,
but all I received was a plastic baggie
full of ash,
swirled through with splinters of bone.

I expected blood,
but all I got was clay
before you melted into the harbor,
thin layers of grit
charcoaling the surface.

That's what death is:
when something pink
wings away into gray.

I saw it—

I saw my reflection in the water,
blotted with pieces of your body—
I was there.

But, still,
every time I swim in the ocean
I look for you
to come singing out of the Sound,
as bright as a scythe
or a bullet rewound back into the chamber,
that flash of gunpowder reversed.

The shine will be so bright
the morning glories will turn to you,
you will shade those cowardly facts,
that reason,
the way it denies things I can feel
in the spiny flaws
that make up my childish heart.

You will be water-stars on my eyelashes,
visible only on the fringe,
you will be whole again,
not pieces in a plastic bag,
you will become a possible thing.

I don't believe in god,
but I believe
in this impossible world.

The way we circle each other like moons,
addicts of hurt held in orbit,
always searching for a green sky.

I can't see the Northern Lights from here,
but I know they exist.

Biding Forward

I live for the moments I get to wait in airports,
live for the liminal space where nothing can be done
but waiting, live for the roaring vacuum of so
many people in between. Today I learned
what a nightingale looks like. Drab. Brown.
Unremarkable. It's like laurel. When I
was a child and I heard *laurel wreath*, I
imagined something swollen with its own beauty,
bursting florality, tipsy with color, recognizably
a winner, honored, whole. But alas, no. Drab.
Green. Unremarkable. Leaves to pick out before
you eat. It's these in between things I love
the most. The dull bird with the full-throated
song, the bored leaves conferring a champion,
the way a bee keeps our whole world pollinated
as it buzzes its innocuous way through a drab,
blue, unremarkable sky. I live for such in between
moments. They say to me: dare to exist
quietly. Dare to not climb the ladder, just because
it's there. Dare to stop dancing if you don't want
to dance. This isn't *Footloose*. This is Bradley
International Airport in Hartford, Connecticut, and all
you can do here is wait for your life to begin,
wait to arrive at a hearth, wait to be welcomed,
wait for someone to see that even as drab
and unremarkable as you may appear, there's so
much more the surface isn't reflecting. Wait.
Be okay with knowing that waiting is a state of being.
Wait. And know that living is the same thing, if
you're willing to wait until you can be honest
with yourself.

Strictly Old Testament

I am stockpiling maps, even now on my own porch, even
now as the squirrels throw their nuts down to bury later,
to eat later, everyone is so good at later and I am only
good at before,

so good at before it's nearly biblical, strictly Old
Testament stuff where it's never about forgiveness but
all about being stuck with each other because everyone
lived hundreds of years, all about Eve who was handing
out fruit to all her sisters, no matter what you heard there
weren't any snakes involved and no way were those apples
red like a Renaissance painting but definitely green,

green apples like I always used to ask for because all the
other apples were red so I always wanted the special ones
but forget the fruit, but anyway,

I'd bet anything Eve was handing out firewood, I bet
she chopped the whole goddamn tree down and started
warming all the people up, started letting them move
forward to the later, to the New Testament stuff where
everyone suddenly believes in later and forgets all the
shallowness of death,

but if I had been Eve's sister I still would be eating all
those unripe fruits, cramping up my small intestine, that
snake still inside me and it tells me things I shouldn't do
like collect maps back to the places and people I should, I
would just, why can't I,

I must let go of the way all those screaming protestors
outside the Planned Parenthood should let go of the Old
Testament and every star-spangled eagle thought they

thought they thought themselves because my god how
am I going to ever see later with a racket like that,
that I can hear even as I pretend having a cold beer on my
porch in the present and writing a poem is a way to see
later and not a cry into a day so hot my skin feels peeled
and I am blinded by another summer where the snake
won't shut its forked tongue smile, where I can't see the
dire, where I can't stop holding on to my maps that plot
my way through worlds I'll never get back,

because I miss everyone and everything even as I see how
later, now, now, how looking forward like everyone else
can is the point, is the thing, is all.

Light

Why do I think I have to use the heavy words,
like "Love" or "Death"?
Can I just tell you a story, instead?

—

This is the first summer I've spent
with my own reflection.
I can no longer see your face
or memorize my own.

A reflection is not company,
nor a semblance,
a reflection is the color white.

—

Penfield Beach is not the kind of seascape
I grew up in—
too stunted, too rocky,
horseshoe crabs like prehistoric beasts.

The emptiness of a shell is a reflection,
an illusion,
something that tricks your belief—
nothing to see here.

I write my name at low tide,
my toes crinkling into mudflat sand,
into wasting.

The foam rests in thin lines,
not water, not air,
but something living.

I efface it,
throw shells back home.

—

So here's the story:

Once upon a time, there was a woman who still called herself a girl, and she was sad. She wanted to put her sadness in a jar, opaque, so no one could see it, and throw it out to sea, away, farther. But she was scared of two things: that someone would find the jar and catch her sadness like a cold, and something worse. The woman-child feared that without her sadness she would not be herself anymore, would be alone with someone she didn't recognize, a horrifying word: transformed.

—

That's as far as the story goes,
real stories don't have endings,
real stories just end.

It's not an uncommon one,
but it's all I have:
white, white, white.

Not empty,
not blank,
not quite,
but the color
that is all the colors combined.

Light.

After, Later, Soon

It's the thing I didn't know about summer, before:
that every day is a day of new flowers.

Fecund New England, California trailing
ghost poppies, death-bloom afterimages
as my eyes find a new sun, new flowers:

papaver orientale, irises, yellow flowers with
flat tops whose names I can't find, am
not sure it would do me better to know.

They are upturned parasols of a lady I never
was, the clotted raptures of the woman I'm
still becoming: louder and more used to taking

up space in this world and lowly and up-reaching
and yours. I used to only dream of elsewhere.
I used to be rapt in only the concept of after,

later, soon. Don't come along slinging bouquets now.
If you leave them in the gardens
we can walk them together, finding new flowers

every day, no longer waiting to become.

A Story

When I first started writing, I never wrote about anything I owned. I made up stories in each and every piece—a collision I'd never been in, a rabbit I'd never seen disemboweled in the snow, pies I'd never tasted—I was, I am, a storyteller. I wanted to be an oracle for the human condition, so I imagined its vista. But I forgot that I too am human. That my condition is also, necessarily, yours. That it shouldn't take a translator the nausea of switching between metaphor and reality to decode your life for you.

What I forgot is this: my stories are enough.

I was scared if I released them, they wouldn't come back to me. But here is my burnt offering: I know, as the Greeks did at Delphi, that what we cinder and char is lost to us. I know now, finally, that that's okay. So I give to you what little I have to give.

I moved into a small apartment with my mother after years of wandering. The house is an exclamatory yellow and together we live on the top floor, a murky mouth of old, splintering wood and niches made for saints. In her niche, my mother keeps me: a Christmas teacup I gave her as a child, a necklace like dewdrops caught in a spiderweb she claims I made, a photograph—always me alone, never us together, never everyone, never my father, never the whole family. I am long past the time to leave the family home—but how can you leave a place that hasn't existed in years? I pay rent here. This is what living alone looks like for me: astringent, constricted back into the womb, no forethought. Only my most masterful of skills: making it up as I go along. My niche holds only books.

Today my mother unpacked a mystery box from our once-was house, our 3,000-miles-away house, never a family home either. Small and heavy and unmarked, it held: a poem about my dead father, a photo of me, and another, never sharing my mother's frame, another and then . . . crackling paper bearing forth tough, lopsided fruits that made my chest a drumskin. Our only family portrait drawn out in sea and stone and varnish.

My first and only real family memories all happen near the water. Most clearly, disposing of his ashes in a harbor. But first, the rocks. We moved to California at the start of my memories, so all I really know of him is collecting rocks from the sand to bring them back to the ocean. They revealed their true natures there—deeper and brighter than what the dry world had made of them. I took them home, but cried when they faded back to dullness. He found a lacquer that made them look wet all the time. My mother put them in a glass bowl once they dried, along with a piece of coral the shape of a heart. Our family captured only once, in inanimate objects my father brought to life. In that way, he made me a writer. That's what I do now: hope against hope the inanimate things I create can live.

I am not trapped in the house my mother and I share. Though I may leave it someday, know this: we share it. Only blocks from the Sound, we split the place that holds him. My mother isn't more sentimental than me, though it seems that way. Our memorials just appear differently: one in shrines, the other in every word she can grab and grub and hold on to.

One idea shoulders past all others: this is what writing is. My story gone, taking up residence in your mind. The one idea I want to leave you with now, even if I lost you in my text, my ramblings, my shrine to memory collapsed in its own smoke, is this:

Your stories are enough too.

HOME

The Beginning of It

I left my blood
in uneven patches
all over Rhode Island.

Sliced the soft, untouched arch of my foot
in the shallows as the boat was brought to dock
and hobbled into a rain-soaked July.

—

Bruises fade more quickly now
that your mouth has moved across my body.

So do bug bites.
So do the blunt pains
of moving through a quiet life.

—

When I wake next to you
in a room with no curtains,
this is what I see:
freckles,
burned in a planetary splay
over shoulders corded with muscle
that move like wings stirring under your skin
when I run my nails up and down your back.

When we brush our teeth together,
side by side in the wide mirror,
reflected is the moment
you put your hand on the small of my back
when you lean over to turn the faucet on.

When we swim in the ocean
on the deserted beach,
bringing cheap beer in the can
out into the frigid water,
my whole head is drowning

in the look of you, in the unwritten moment
you emerge right next to me,

the cold no longer circling my ribcage.

—

You are giving me something,
and you don't even know it.
You are enough—it takes no toll on you.

—

Later, reading
in the grass by the salt pond,
the wound beneath me reopens.

It will reopen again and again.

I know we are standing on top of the headland
and deciding whether or not to jump.

I know I am bleeding.
But I don't want to rewrite anything.
I don't want memory to have to suffice for you.

I don't want to imagine the poem of my life.

I want to reopen my wounds again and again,
knowing they heal faster in your company,

limping into August,
hoping for September,

my blood uneven heel prints on sandy ground.

Old Silver Beach

There are lighthouses distant
and dune roses cluster
against the wooly whorls
of sand. It is softer here
than the places my mind
grasps at, sighing after.

Imagine to be unkissed again.
To be a morning glory
opening to the sun's keen
attention for the first time.
To be this beach, protean
planes swept clean and even.

It is beyond imagining, so
much to come later but also
the idea of nothing before.

The constant attrition of even
these breathing waves.

The consistency of knowing
we have lost again, will keep
losing, are lost.

The nervy effort of watching
a peach bud open, knowing
it can never close again.

At 7 a.m. it is warm enough
to sit with my legs bare
on the boardwalk's edge.
No fog today, and you
somewhere before me,
somewhere in this endless,
unimaginable universe, you.

Somewhere dune roses turn
their heads to the lighthouse
beams again and again
and again.

Not Fallow, No

I like being with you,
              even when it rains.
Like has all the softness
              of a word whose single syllable
              is sieving out what you really mean to say.
I have been places—
              I have seen foxglove and hibiscus bloom
              and eaten many kinds of bread at many tables
              and made a processional of my life.
                       It's not that I wanted more,
                       it's that I have always been hungry
                                and I've always been hungering
                                for something the world wouldn't
                                                 hand over.
That's all.
              The places I've been have been lavender,
              if you know what I mean.
All of them, well, you've been able to find
              good coffee
                       but, there's still
                       that kind of vaudeville act
                       that happens in new places
                       where the places impress you
                                for only so long.
Today, I am in Rhode Island.
              It is not Hawaii or London
              or Chicago or the South of France
              or even Washington in spring—none.
I don't feel like this is a place that knows
              other places exist
                       or cares much that they do.
The fogmist is weaving through the rain,
rising off Ninigret Pond and into our bedroom
                                (I left the porch door open
                                in the night)
and you are still asleep, all stubble and
              quiet knowing in your drowsy head.

There is (what I could swear up and down
                and side to side)
a World's Tree in my direct line of vision
                            (in the few years you've brought
                            me here I could swear
                            it's grown despite the salt)
and a swath of garden that in July
                will be all bees and roses that somehow
                smell like the none-too-distant sea,
but in early April is still the umber and russet
                of fallow farmland.
                            Not fallow, no.
If you gave me a nickel for every time
                I had been somewhere else
                but without even knowing it
                            really wanted to be here
we'd fill the pond twice over in clichés.
So this morning I'll get up
                and make the good coffee we bought down the
street
and write poems while you sleep—
                            using words too imprecise
                            like

                poets tend to do
                while outside it doesn't rain,
                            it pours
                                    into a pond where
                the circles ripple ever inward—always
                            back to you.

Things I Learned in Rhode Island

Many, many bird calls.
How to spend whole days
without makeup. What you're like
when you're actually relaxed.

That many, many jellyfish gather
in the salt pond. How good it feels
to shower outside
after a day of salt and sand.
What kinds of sandwiches keep best
in the cooler for hours.

Many, many drinking games:
dice, the stump game, that Pokémon one.
How it feels to wake up next to you.
What you're like when you're drunk.

That many, many sunsets and sunrises
and fireworks can make you feel like
you've already known someone a lifetime.
How to let my hair grow out,
whites glimmering metallic in the sun.
What you're like
when you're badly hungover.

Many, many ways to make eggs
so everyone's happy.
How to almost
drown in the breakers.
What it feels like to be saved.

That many, many songs are best sung
at the top of your lungs. How deeply
you care for the people you care for,
so everyone's having fun.
What having fun without anxiety
feels like.

Many, many ways to remove a tick.
How to find the dock. What it feels like
to have you beside me in the water—
safe.

That many, many birds call your home
their home,
herons like question marks roosting
on the sandbar.
How much I like the little things:
making coffee with you,
the way you smile in your sleep,
your sun freckles.
What happens when
you don't wear water shoes.

Many, many ways
to get a television
to work.
How to
dance
in the rain.
What home feels like.

That there are many,
many things that make me
love you.
How to let someone
save you.
What I really want
in life is simple:
to be here,
with you.

On Our Way

Trains aren't for falling in love.
That's in films where the titles
run too long and the heroine
isn't a hero by any definition
but a point of interest
on a very boring map.

Trains are for finding love's depth,
for realizations of love,
for reading new books
and getting sick from sitting backward
and finding an excess of love's
surprise fervor.

If I were a bird, not a pigeon
but something larger and angrier
and more rangy, not a pigeon
but a robin's-egg-blue bird,
I wouldn't have needed to take a train
to reach such foregone conclusions.

Birds love the sky in a way
that some would call a fool's
leap of faith—the cistern of air
holds no surprises for them,
because to know something fully
is to find all the big-talk stuff
is little-talk, to find a fissure
in the lining.

When all is above ground,
there is nothing to pray for anymore
and that is love.

Unbidden and full.

But we are not birds,
we are humans who have to,
sometimes, take trains
sometimes, shuttling between
our smaller town and larger cities,
sometimes we have to have
the monotonous rail clack train track
endless hunger to move forward.
Before I loved you, I knew I could.

Not because of some new turned
page in my biography or a romantic
moon-bath of a night or even
the domesticity of buying groceries
but because of a train ride
where I read *Brave New World*
out loud to you.

Quietly, quietly, so the strangeness
didn't rend the small, windburned
worlds of the other passengers asunder.

Quietly, quietly, so you had to
lean in to hear me.

I have loved you now for what,
in bird years, must seem like
an amethyst-colored forever,
a sunset streaked with sea salt
where the sun never sets.

We have done things
to each other.

We have hurt each other badly,
leaving the one that did the hurting
perhaps more broken than
the receiver of said hurt.

I have sometimes forgotten
how to be loving, maybe,
have sometimes found myself
nauseous and looking backward
at a landscape I didn't recognize.

But then, out of the fogmist,
a train comes.

A train comes to take us home, again,
and I cry on the train but,
I promise you,
the details don't matter.

I am not a hero
and I am not a bird
and I am not a passing point of interest
on a map.

I am a girl on a train
with a boy she loves
and he's hurt and has hurt her
and I am crying not because
of all that
but because this train
is my sky.

I live on this train now,
moving forever forward,
and each view out each window
is another one of you.

As You Do, As I Do

Your wrist bones cracking cold on the walk from the
subway, The Met opened its doors just for us that
morning with its steps clean and the great hall's sloe-
eyed reeds still nodding drowsy in their tall, stately urns
and watching half-lidded as we checked our coats and
I dragged you to my favorite room before the crowds
could come to the bright, echoing chamber that withheld
its echoes and gave us silence and a photograph of my
silhouetted figure against Central Park behind the glass
stretched like membranes three stories tall and I couldn't
help but feel breathless there with you between those
ancient stones,

obelisks just how van Gogh described his Cypresses as
if knowing how they would become a church, reside as a
shrine to beauty and what I really want to talk about is
the way your face looked viewing those trees—I can only
describe it as someone who loves unique, beautiful things
(even if they've been loved by others before) as if they're
always seeing them for the first time, as if you went with
Theo to clear out his brother's rooms to find the painter's
real bones, gold spilled eye to canvas in the cellar and

later, when you took my picture again, framed by some
dream of dreams by Kiefer, I turned around into you,
holding your phone and seeing me through it, seeing me
in the art and I could understand what it would mean to
see the world like that, that it is to love it and not just in
a call and response kind of way, but to know real beauty is
like real love—endlessly renewing, surprisingly alive, and
a bleeding paint kind of true: it is not just saying I love
you too, but rather seeing the beloved fully, and always
again as if for the first time.

Goldfinch in the Snow

You are the one thing I want to write of
and the one thing I don't have words for.
You are too much, suffice to say
that you are a quick, bright, laughing thing
whose wing prints can be found all over
the inner hollows of my body.
I have been washed and cleaned
and been made ready, inside but also
out: I have washed my makeup off
and let my hair dry to its whitening roots
in the clear sea air. We wake up
to snow this morning—a late April's Fool
hushing an already quiet place.
No birds today except the way your
lips brush over mine, naked pink
and electrically charged in flight.
I am still watching for birds outside
and though I never know which are which,
does it matter? Does it matter that to me
their songs are just noises in the predawn
mirror light if I look for them in the snow?
I'm not too proud to tell you
that I brandish a pen as communion,
that I use only what I have at my disposal
because I am not a girl who
is often handed over anything else.
So believe me when I say I saw a goldfinch
in the early April snow, believe me
when I say he came when my eyes
opened on you beside me in bed,
believe me when I tell you that the morning
glories didn't freeze and shrivel but turned
their heads when you opened your eyes, too...

The pet names the French use,
they don't translate. *My cabbage,*
my little weasel. I wonder if in Provence,
if in that lemon light, those cherry,
snowless mornings, that my wordless mouth
could maybe translate this instead:
my words, my poem,
my goldfinch in the snow?

Daucus Carota

I want to know the names of all the flowers,
and I want to give them to you.

Not the flowers, but something more permanent:
the wellspring of knowledge seems to be knowing
things for what they really are.

We took the dog hiking at the reservoir—
his beseeching whines in the car, the light
from the water playing across my closed eyelids—
and I saw a white flower I knew.

It's Queen Anne's Lace, I told you.

You let me tell my story: Once upon a time,
I took a boat to a small island off the coast
of France. It used to be a prison, but these days
there's only a short tour and in between the old
stone ruins, swales of Queen Anne's Lace.
I had never seen it before, somehow, its ruffled
circle, a doily, a cluster of flowers flat and tall,
waiting for someone taller to look down to see
its perfect whorling.

I was with another boy that day, one that would leave me.

Later, you would bring me a sprig from our
neighborhood, sweaty from the humidity
of a New England summer: *Queen Anne's Lace,*
you'd say. A lullaby, a promise, a kiss.

—

As a poet, I deal in flowers,
as a doctor, you deal in bodies.

You want to know the names of all the bones,
muscles, organs, all the ways they can break
and dilate and rot.
We both need a kind of scriptorium, just
like Virginia Woolf said: a room for not just
words, but designations, categorizations,
the hard-hearted look at the world that lets us
take it in through small, needful gasps.

I went to see the Bodies Exhibit
to try to learn what you saw in the human form,
and was met with a field of blooms:

the brain a clumping of Hydrangeas, the bisected
lung a flattened Hibiscus, the carefully picked
apart arteries and capillaries a cinnabar show,
a bloody Queen Anne's Lace.

The fetal development room full of buds unopened,
many-layered Ranunculus-stained sacs in utero,
a night's green expanse full of small, singular Jasmine
blossom, Tuberose, Angel's Trumpet.

My map of the Science Center filled with marginalia:
Amaryllis bowels, Calendula ovaries, Monk's Head
tongues.

An entire garden to bring back to you.

—

The heat lightning this summer appeals to us both:
poetry and science in encore after encore of light
without the fanfare, the thunder too far away to wake
the dog, sleeping here, on top of both our feet on the porch.

We are both reading, and here's the apologia of our
whole love: you turn to me to tell me what you've
learned.

That Queen Anne's Lace is really *Daucus Carota* or
Wild Carrot, an edible plant also called Bishop's Lace
or even Bird's Nest.

And I, in turn, remember a book of narrative poetry
from my childhood: pioneers had to be careful, for
Wild Carrot and Hemlock are nearly identical if
you're not sure what to look for.

The right plant is the perfect companion to your
other flowers, helps attract pollinators, a weed,
but one people are happy to see, beautiful
and beneficial even as it takes over and seeps
into your landscape.

The other is much the same, besides the death.

We both look at the bloom you brought me
and decide together what we can't really know,
but decide to believe in: *Daucus Carota*,
something the same for both of us,
in verse and in truth.

May I

Spring won't come outside, so we bring
the April showers in, their rhyme
creating blossoms for our carpet,
the dog sneezing snowdrop and daffodil
and tulip pollen in his doleful, doggy
way. Why demure? Why perhaps? Why
wait for the things we want? All this soil
on the hardwood may not be clean,
but the way I feel when you touch me
in this rain is dazzling, dazzling.
The wren perched on our lamp warbles,
and the ropes of the winter of the mind
fall away. Even the night forgets
blackness here. March, its hoary frosts
and sharp edges, me, my insecurities
and anxieties, you, your overthinking
and reserve. Spring won't come outside,
so we bloom inside: dazzled, dazzled
by the budding, steady beats of
our own two hearts in tandem.

White Witch Moth

Science can't tell us
why moths fly toward our lights,
not for sure.

But we humans,
we don't need to be sure,
we need only to recognize bewilderment
to know the truth:
we're fucking up the wild with our glow.

Creating mirages that must seem miracles,
the moon finally found after all that trembling.

Who are we to do to them
what we do to ourselves?

Putting out sugar
for hummingbirds in feeders
like red, long-throated flowers,
faux tangerines in a blue glass bowl
on my counter telling you

I am a good woman,
nurturing,
I will feed you

with all this honey
in little bear figures,
the bear letting you know
I could have harvested it all myself.

We are liars.
I am a liar.

A mustard plant may bloom,
but it is not a sunflower.
All light can be bright,
but all lights don't serve the same purpose.

The hospital fluorescents flicker
on off on off.
I am waiting to know
if we have time yet
to make my lies into something like reality.

The thunder that is not thunder,
but the blare of some television
pinches me awake.
The pine scent that is not trees,
but disinfectant,
leaves me shaking.

I could be your good woman.
I could be nurturing.
I could be both the bouquet
and the rose bush,
if only I am given the time to become.

—

The moon's uprising path,
the white witch moth
like a crane reaching upward,
the light-soaked moment
where my wings—
the largest wings in the world—
carry me not away,

but home to you.

The Spine Remembers Wings

after Larry Levis

I'm still trying to map out Connecticut,
    to even find it on the map.
        I am many things here: a daughter, a girlfriend,
    a family, a poet, a mother to a small, furry
    beast, an asylum unto myself.
            But this place seems more a self-effacing slate—
            not safe haven but exile, not specific
            but a general feeling of the Christmas trees
            left out for the garbageman on the side of the road.
So I read about the place.
    I try to dig out its dead blooms,
    try to build a cathedral out of its pretty,
    generic skies—can you build up luster
    where there's only surface?
            Even the state bird is a waste.
            A robin? I read an entire book
            on robins, looking for anything that
            could make me feel at home.
                All I know now is that their babies
                have many names: pullet, colt, jake.
                This seems to be more unsaying
                than saying anything at all.
So I hike the state,
risk frostbite to try to find
what gives this place a face,
a soul, anything like a self.
    But what I see is trees I can't name,
    fish I call trout even though they're probably
    every other species, birds above me
    riderless and floating in the dawn.
            It's not that it can't be beautiful here,
            whatever that word means, it's just
            that if I were Penelope at her loom,
            I wouldn't be sure how to mark that
            yes, this story takes place in Connecticut.
                Yes, we were here and could only have ever
                been here.

Instead I have
    the way you bring me coffee while I
    write this poem, your hand, finger to thumb,
    circling my waist and making me feel as small
    and soft as a jake, and maybe even as safe.
        The dog has fallen back asleep, but
        if I'm being honest, sitting here in silence
        seems to be its own place on the map.
           The kind of map where only we could find
each other,
        where the spine has at least a chance at
remembering
          wings.

The Constant State of Being

I have been dreaming of your shoulders
five years now, since I first saw your
stars. The broad sea, speckled
as a whale shark and I plunged
in, unafraid of depths or diving,
or trying not to be as you threw
your body over mine. Shelter,
asylum, opus of kisses and tea
drank while it rains—the black
honey spooned into the voices
and voiceless alike. Each
night I climb the stairs
to the sky itself, cleaving the heavens
with what can no longer
be called trespass. As much as
we can own each other, you
are mine and I yours. I come
to you, barefoot and bleeding,
and you cauterize my wounds
with song—heady, sweet,
and low, as it makes the freckles
on your back dance, narrow
wings folding and unfolding.
Near the water, a hibiscus unfurls,
its stamens clotted with gold,
releasing more stars into
our sky. Beside me, your
stars twitch, your eyelids. What
are you dreaming, now, love?
Of what beginning? There are
no endings here.

Acknowledgments

As this book is more of an autobiography than anything else, I have an entire lifetime of people to thank, but I'll start with these few.

Gratefully acknowledged are the following publications, where particular poems appeared in earlier versions: *Necessary Fiction* for their publication of "The Face of God"; *Sixfold* for their publication of "Careful Cartography," "Gardening," "Forgiveness," "Grocery Shopping with You," and "The Beginning of It"; and *The Graveyard Zine* for their publication of "Things My Mother Taught Me."

Dr. Ross Tangedal and the amazing student staff at Cornerstone Press deserve special mention for their incredible work on this manuscript—this book is all the better for the time they gave it. Thank you for putting your hearts into this. And special thanks to Maddy Firth for her beautiful artwork, which she so generously granted permission to use.

Thank you to my blood family and my chosen family for their unending support and belief, which includes anyone with the last name Bohm, Mahony, Bonet, Bridge, Stramoski, Infante, Wookey, and Mendel.

My writing family at Smith and Fairfield encouraged me and challenged me in equal measure, specifically: Ellen Doré Watson, Carol Ann Davis, Annie Boutelle, Michael White, Hollis Seamon, Rachel Basch, Stephanie Harper,

Allison Wagner, Tommy Hahn, Scott Schilling, and Dan Hajducky.

My friends don't necessarily care quite as much about poetry, but they have always cheered me on anyway: Rosa Town, Cait Hartney, Jade Stuart, Nicole Edry, Becky Reindel, Amanda Goodwin, Meghan Russell and Trevor Milward, Kayleigh and Andrew Mann, Linda and Dan Torv, and all my UO work wives. I am so lucky to have each of you in my corner.

Thank you to my best friend and biggest cheerleader, my mother, Teresa Moynihan Bohm. I wouldn't exist (and neither would this book) without your love, bravery, and kindness.

And lastly, to the love of my life, Forrest Mahony. Thank you so much for bringing me home.

DEVON BOHM is a writer, poet, and educator. She holds degrees from Smith College and Fairfield University, and her work has appeared in *Labrys*, *The Graveyard Zine*, *Necessary Fiction*, *Spry*, and *Sixfold*. She received the Hatfield Prize for Best Short Story 2011, an honorable mention in the L. Ron Hubbard Writers of the Future Contest Third Quarter 2020, and a place on the long-list for *Wigleaf*s Top Very Short Fictions 2021. She lives in West Hartford, Connecticut.